OCT 1 1 2006

PUBLIC LIBRARY, DISTRICT OF COLUMBIA

W9-CHV-590

WE THE PEOPLE

Fort Sumter

by Michael Burgan

Content Adviser: Kurt Hackemer, Ph.D.,
Department of History
University of South Dakota

Reading Adviser: Rosemary G. Palmer, Ph.D.,
Department of Literacy, College of Education
Boise State University

COMPASS POINT BOOKS
MINNEAPOLIS, MINNESOTA

Compass Point Books
3109 West 50th Street, #115
Minneapolis, MN 55410

Visit Compass Point Books on the Internet at *www.compasspointbooks.com*
or e-mail your request to *custserv@compasspointbooks.com*

On the cover: A Currier & Ives print of the bombardment of Fort Sumter, Charleston Harbor

Photographs ©: Library of Congress, front cover, back cover, 14, 16, 17, 20, 25, 27, 30, 34, 35;
Prints Old and Rare, back cover (far left); North Wind Picture Archives, 4, 8, 9, 19, 21, 26, 33, 40;
U.S. Senate Collection/Abraham Lincoln by Freeman Thorp, 5; National Baseball Hall of Fame
Library/MLB Photos via Getty Images, 7; MPI/Getty Images, 11, 13, 32; Stock Montage, Inc., 12;
The Granger Collection, New York, 15, 23, 29, 39; Time Life Pictures/National Archives/Getty
Images, 31; NARA, 36; Corbis, 37; Bob Krist/Corbis, 41.

Editor: Julie Gassman
Page Production: The Design Lab
Photo Researcher: Marcie C. Spence
Cartographer: XNR Productions, Inc.
Library Consultant: Kathleen Baxter

Creative Director: Keith Griffin
Editorial Director: Carol Jones
Managing Editor: Catherine Neitge

Library of Congress Cataloging-in-Publication Data
Burgan, Michael.
  Fort Sumter / by Michael Burgan.
     p. cm.—(We the people)
  Includes bibliographical references and index.
  ISBN 0-7565-1629-3 (hardcover)
  1. Fort Sumter (Charleston, S.C.)—Siege, 1861—Juvenile literature. 2. Charleston (S.C.)—
History—Civil War, 1861-1865—Juvenile literature. 3. United States—History—Civil War,
1861-1865—Causes—Juvenile literature. I. Title. II. We the people (Series) (Compass Point Books)
  E471.1.B87 2006
  973.7'31—dc22   2005025081

Copyright © 2006 by Compass Point Books
All rights reserved. No part of this book may be reproduced without written permission from the publisher. The publisher
takes no responsibility for the use of any of the materials or methods described in this book, nor for the products thereof.
Printed in the United States of America.

TABLE OF CONTENTS

FIRST BATTLE OF THE CIVIL WAR

Above the harbor of Charleston, South Carolina, a single shell exploded. Its orange glow filled the early morning sky of April 12, 1861. Soon more shells flew across the harbor.

Incoming shells started fires in the fort, and smoke filled the air.

4

The target was Fort Sumter, a thick-walled fortress sitting on an island. Inside the fort were Union soldiers. For months, they had survived inside the fort with little food. Their mission was to defend Fort Sumter as long as they could.

The shells falling around and inside the fort came from the artillery of the Confederate Army. The Confederacy was a group of Southern states that seceded, or broke away, from the United States. These states believed U.S. President Abraham Lincoln was a threat to their rights under the U.S. Constitution. They feared

President Abraham Lincoln

5

he would try to end slavery, which was legal at the time. Seceding, the Confederates thought, was the only way to protect their rights.

For months, Southern leaders had demanded that the Union troops leave Fort Sumter, which they had occupied since December 1860. These leaders claimed that the Confederacy, which included South Carolina, was now a separate country and the U.S. government had no right to keep troops on Confederate land. Like President James Buchanan who served before him, Lincoln refused to move the troops. Now the South's army was trying to take the fort.

Captain Abner Doubleday was a Union officer inside Fort Sumter. He later wrote about the attack. When the Confederate shells, "after sailing high in the air, came down … and buried themselves in the … ground, their explosion shook the fort like an earthquake." As the morning went on, Union troops fired Fort Sumter's large guns back at the Confederate artillery surrounding them. The

6

Union, however, began to run out of shells and gunpowder. Their troops soon agreed to turn over the fort to the Confederacy.

The U.S. government and the Southern states had failed to settle their differences. The two sides were now caught in a civil war, beginning with the attack on Fort Sumter. The

Captain Abner Doubleday

leaders of the Confederate states said they were battling to defend rights guaranteed to them under the Constitution. But President Lincoln said the Southern states did not have a legal right to secede. He believed the U.S. government

7

had to keep the Union whole, even though it led to war.

The Civil War continued until 1865. It was the bloodiest war the United States has ever fought, with 1.1 million soldiers killed or wounded. But the North's victory kept the country together, as Lincoln had hoped. The war also freed more than 4 million African-American slaves.

After the Civil War ended, newly freed slaves traveled to the North on ships.

TROUBLES BETWEEN THE NORTH AND SOUTH

The fighting at Fort Sumter had deep roots. For more than 70 years, Northerners and Southerners had argued about slavery. In general, people from the Southern states favored slavery, while many Northerners opposed it. Southern plantation owners relied on African-American slaves to raise their crops and work as servants in their homes.

Slaves load cotton onto ships in New Orleans, Louisiana.

9

Many small farm owners used slave labor as well. Slaves also lived in towns and cities and worked in places like shipyards and mills. The Southern economy was deeply tied to slavery.

Northern states had outlawed slavery, although free blacks in the North could not vote or send their children to school with whites. Some Northerners opposed slavery because they felt the unequal treatment of blacks was unfair. But many others were opposed to slavery for economic reasons. They were concerned, for example, that slaves took jobs from white workers.

Some Northerners wanted to abolish, or get rid of, slavery right away. Others wanted to restrict its growth into new areas. They believed slavery should not be allowed in new states and territories as they joined the Union.

Slave owners believed if the citizens of the new states and territories wanted slavery, it should be allowed. The U.S. Constitution allowed slavery and did not give the national government direct power to limit it. During the

Northerners held antislavery rallies like this one in Boston, Massachusetts, in 1835.

late 1700s and early 1800s, however, Congress had passed laws that placed limits on the growth of slavery in new states and territories. By the 1850s, fewer Southerners wanted limits on slavery. At the same time, Northerners' opposition to slavery grew.

During the U.S. presidential election of 1860, slavery was the main issue. Abraham Lincoln was the Republican candidate. This party had strong support in the North and none in the South. The Republicans did not want slavery to

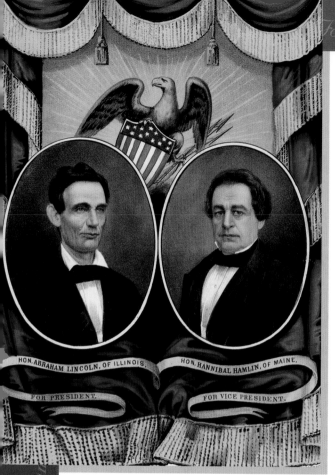

A campaign poster of the Republican candidates for president and vice president in 1860

spread into any new territories.

Their main opponents were the Democrats, who were divided over the question of slavery in new territories. Northern Democrats believed the settlers of new territories should decide themselves, while the territory was being organized, whether or not slavery should be legal there. Most Northern Democrats believed that slavery would not expand into Western territories because more settlers from "free states" were moving west than from slave states. These initial settlers could take measures to keep slavery out.

Southern Democrats, meanwhile, said slave owners had a right to bring their slaves into the new territories. They argued that territories should be settled and ready

12

In an 1860 political cartoon, the Republican "train" is set to split the Democratic party in two.

to become a state before deciding whether or not to allow slavery. This gave slave owners time to settle in the new area, increasing the likelihood that the territory would become a slave state. The two Democratic sides could not agree, so each side ran their own candidate in the election.

On November 6, Lincoln won the election. He tried to assure Southerners that he and his party would not end slavery everywhere in the United States. Some Southerners, however, worried that the Republicans would not keep this promise.

SOUTH CAROLINA SECEDES

Just days after Lincoln's victory, voters in South Carolina took action. They made plans to hold a convention in December to discuss seceding from the Union. For years, the state's lawmakers had strongly defended slavery, and some had threatened to secede when they thought the U.S. government was unfairly limiting their state's rights.

In 1836, for example, one South Carolina lawmaker

South Carolinians met on November 12, 1860, to ask the state legislature to hold a special convention to discuss seceding from the Union.

said, "I will go home to preach … disunion, and civil war" if Congress tried to pass a law against slavery. That spirit was stronger than ever in November 1860. A female slave owner from South Carolina wrote in her diary, "We [should] all lay down our lives, sooner than free our slaves in our midst."

A poster to announce that South Carolina had seceded from the Union.

On December 20, 1860, South Carolina's voters said they could not accept a president "whose opinions and purposes are hostile to slavery." South Carolina declared that it was now an independent state, no longer part of the United States. In Charleston, the state's major city, people celebrated in the streets when they heard the news.

15

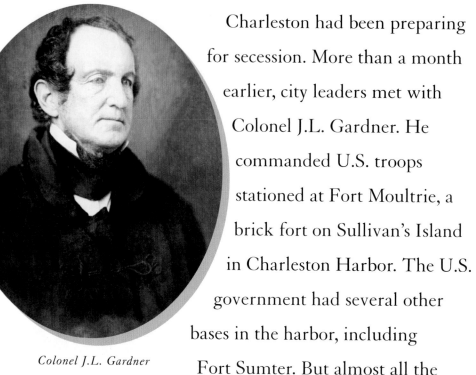

Colonel J.L. Gardner

Charleston had been preparing for secession. More than a month earlier, city leaders met with Colonel J.L. Gardner. He commanded U.S. troops stationed at Fort Moultrie, a brick fort on Sullivan's Island in Charleston Harbor. The U.S. government had several other bases in the harbor, including Fort Sumter. But almost all the U.S. troops in Charleston were at Fort Moultrie. The Charleston officials told Colonel Gardner that they would not allow any reinforcements to come to Sullivan's Island.

At the same time, the soldiers at the fort knew Charleston residents were angry about Lincoln's election. They heard talk about secession. Gardner and his men began to keep weapons handy, in case anyone tried to attack Fort Moultrie.

GROWING CRISIS IN CHARLESTON

By the time South Carolina seceded, Major Robert Anderson was in command at Fort Moultrie. He was a Southerner who had served at the fort before. He was assigned to the fort in hopes that he could build good relations with the people of Charleston. But Anderson opposed secession, and he was ready to do his job.

President Buchanan, who would remain in office until Lincoln's inauguration in January, ordered Anderson to avoid violence and

Major Robert Anderson

17

protect his men. But if the South Carolina militia attacked, Anderson was to defend himself. Yet he had fewer than 100 men, and the fort was close to some hills. Enemy attackers on the hills could easily fire into the fort. Anderson wrote a friend, "If attacked in force by any one not a simpleton, there is scarcely a [chance] of our being able to hold out."

After South Carolina seceded, the residents of Charleston began to train their own troops. They were preparing to take control of three of the U.S. forts in their harbor. Francis Pickens, governor of South Carolina, had the power to create and use an army if the U.S. government threatened his state.

Major Anderson knew his troops would soon be threatened. By Christmas Day, he decided to take action. South Carolina's military forces would have a much harder time attacking Fort Sumter than Fort Moultrie. It was larger than Fort Moultrie and farther from land. The next evening, Anderson began to ship his troops and supplies to

Before Anderson and his men left Fort Moultrie, they spiked the fort's cannons so they no longer worked properly.

Fort Sumter. He also had to ferry over the families of the soldiers who lived at Fort Moultrie. They moved quickly, before officials in Charleston could figure out what Anderson was doing and try to stop his boats. By the afternoon of December 27, the troops and civilians were safely at Fort Sumter.

The news of Anderson's move upset leaders in South Carolina as well as in Washington, D.C. President Buchanan told several Southern lawmakers that he had not ordered the move. In fact, he had promised Governor

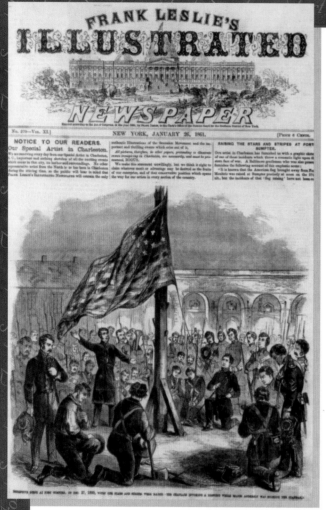

FRANK LESLIE'S ILLUSTRATED NEWSPAPER

No. 279—Vol. XI.] NEW YORK, JANUARY 26, 1861. [Price 6 Cents.

NOTICE TO OUR READERS.

On December 27, Major Anderson raised the American flag at Fort Sumter while the chaplain said a blessing.

Pickens that he would not send reinforcements or move troops to Fort Sumter. But the move was so popular with Northerners that Buchanan did not order Anderson to leave the fort.

Back at the fort, two angry South Carolina officials came to talk to Anderson. They accused him of breaking the president's promise. The major explained that he had feared being attacked if he stayed at Fort Moultrie. He simply wanted to avoid violence. The officials told him to return to Fort Moultrie. Anderson said, "I cannot and will not go back." Now the chances that war would erupt in Charleston Harbor seemed greater than ever.

PREPARING FOR BATTLE

Governor Pickens soon sent Southern troops to Fort
Moultrie and Castle Pinckney, another U.S. military base
in the harbor. Slaves were sent to Moultrie to build up
its walls and move guns. The South Carolinians moved
artillery to other spots in the harbor. By early January, the

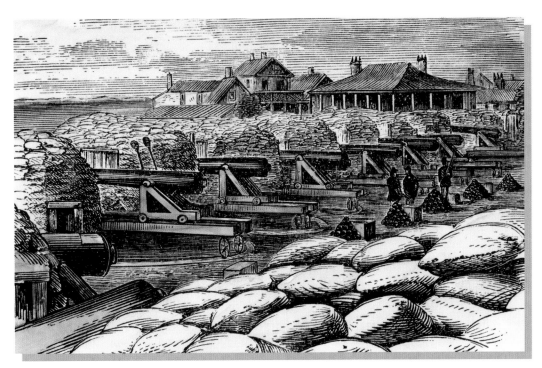

*The South Carolinians used sandbags to build a position
for their artillery at Fort Moultrie.*

21

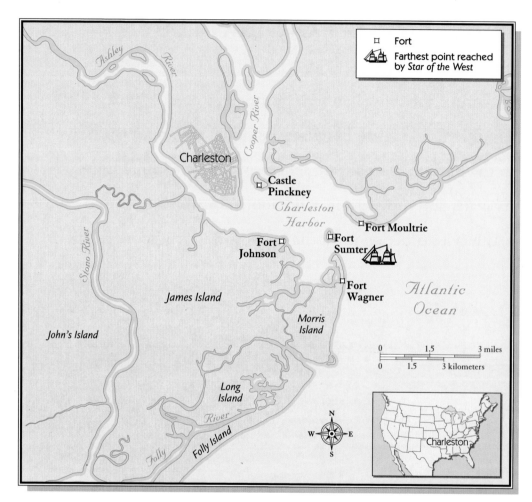

From their position in the middle of the harbor, the Union soldiers at Fort Sumter could easily view surrounding land.

soldiers at Fort Sumter could see the work going on

around them. They guessed that U.S. ships carrying

reinforcements or food would be shot at upon sailing into

Charleston Harbor. The Confederates, Captain Abner Doubleday said, wanted to "force us ... to surrender for lack of supplies."

On January 9, a Union ship tried to sneak into Charleston Harbor. Newspapers in both New York and Charleston, however, had already reported that the *Star of the West* was on its way. Although he heard the reports, Anderson did not believe that the *Star of the West* was coming. As the ship approached Fort Moultrie, Southern artillery shells blasted all around it, with one shell hitting

The *Star of the West* *was fired upon before it even entered the harbor.*

23

the ship. Not willing to enter into battle, Anderson did not allow his troops to fight back.

The *Star of the West* turned around and left Charleston without reaching Fort Sumter. A local newspaper wrote that the attack "was the opening of the ball of revolution. We are proud that our harbor has been so honored."

Inside Fort Sumter, the troops continued to prepare for battle. The U.S. government had started building the fort in 1829, but it was never finished. The men added brick to walls and moved cannons into position. The barracks were not complete, so the soldiers' families slept on mats.

As January went on, the fort began to run low on food. Anderson ordered the families to return to the mainland. The soldiers, who remained, ate salted pork and thick crackers called hardtack. At times, they fished in the harbor for their meals.

Some help arrived on January 31. A friend of Anderson's received permission to come to the island. By boat, he brought beef and vegetables. A few days later,

The families wave goodbye to the soldiers at Fort Sumter as they travel to New York on the ship Marion.

another boat arrived with more food. But on the whole, the hardworking men ate much less than they needed to remain strong. Many became ill as the winter dragged on.

In Washington, Congress tried to end the crisis. Hoping for a compromise on the slavery issue, a special

25

committee of lawmakers wanted to pass a law that protected slavery where it already existed but kept it from expanding into new territories.

Many Southerners, however, were tired of the talk in Washington. By February, six other Southern states had joined South Carolina and seceded from the Union. Mississippi, Florida, Alabama, Georgia, Louisiana, and Texas united to form a new nation: the Confederate

The Confederate states and when they seceded

26

States of America. Four more states—Virginia, Arkansas, Tennessee, and North Carolina—would eventually join the Confederacy.

Jefferson Davis, a senator from Mississippi, was elected president of the Confederacy. In late February, he ordered General P.G.T. Beauregard to take charge of the troops in Charleston. By now, the Confederates feared the Union would send a fleet of ships and many soldiers to help defend Fort Sumter.

Confederate President Jefferson Davis was inaugurated in Montgomery, Alabama, on February 18, 1861.

LAST DAYS OF PEACE

On March 4, 1861, Abraham Lincoln officially became president of the United States. That same day, he received a report from Major Anderson. The men at Fort Sumter would run out of supplies in six weeks. They would need 20,000 troops to defend the fort from a Confederate attack.

At the time, the entire Union Army only had 16,000 men, and most of them were stationed west of the Mississippi River. Lincoln knew he risked a Confederate attack even if he only sent supplies to the fort. The South claimed that Fort Sumter belonged to the Confederacy.

Most of Lincoln's advisers recommended abandoning Fort Sumter to the Confederacy. When a vote was taken in Lincoln's Cabinet, only one member voted to protect the fort. But other Republican leaders told Lincoln to "use all the means in his power to hold and protect the public property of the United States."

As March went on, anger in the South grew. More

slave states considered joining the Confederacy. In early
April, Lincoln finally decided to send reinforcements and
supplies to the fort. If the Confederates attacked, then he
would have an excuse to use military force against the
South. The Confederate states had broken the law by
seceding. President Lincoln had a duty to keep the country

In an 1861 political cartoon, Southerners are set to fall after seceding from the Union.

29

Major Anderson's command was featured on the cover of Harper's Weekly, *a leading newspaper.*

together. But he did not want to fire the first shot.

Anderson was unhappy when he heard Lincoln's plan. He knew the Confederates would attack Fort Sumter and that his men would be surrounded by Confederate fire. Even the incoming reinforcements would not be enough help. The major knew war was about to begin. He wrote to a friend, "I fear that its results cannot fail to be disastrous to all concerned."

Southern leaders soon learned about the Northern ships heading to Charleston. On April 11, Confederate General Beauregard sent three messengers to Fort Sumter. They told Major Anderson that an attack would soon begin unless Anderson turned over the fort. Anderson refused.

Confederate General P.G.T. Beauregard

SHOTS OVER THE HARBOR

The sky was still dark on the morning of April 12 when Confederate guns began to boom. Inside Fort Sumter, however, the men had run out of oil for their lamps. Without lamps, the soldiers were unable to load their guns or fire their artillery. They had to wait for daylight.

The Confederates placed guns all around the harbor. Most of them were at Fort Moultrie. Others sat on a

*A print by Currier & Ives shows the Confederates'
position as they attacked Fort Sumter.*

wooden barge that the Confederates had built just for this battle. Beauregard called his artillery the "circle of fire."

Many residents of Charleston heard the attack start. They came out with picnic baskets and sat on rooftops so they could see the battle. Mary Chesnut lived in Charleston at the time. She wrote, "We hear nothing, can listen to nothing: boom, boom, goes the cannon all the time."

Some South Carolinians wept as they watched the battle.

As the sun rose, Anderson and his men began to fight back. As cannonballs flew around them, they brought out their own shells and gunpowder. The Union's artillery, however, had little effect on the Confederates' equipment or position. The Confederates had strengthened the walls at Fort Moultrie and covered some of their guns with iron

A Currier & Ives illustration shows the smoke-filled interior of the fort.

to make them more resistant to damage.

Meanwhile, several fires raged inside Fort Sumter. Thick smoke made it hard for the soldiers to see or breathe. Captain Doubleday later said they fought amidst "the roaring and crackling of the flames, the dense masses of whirling smoke, the bursting of the enemy's shells." The soldiers were weak from lack of food. And as the day continued, they began running out of gunpowder and shells. There was additional ammunition at the fort, but it was blocked by fire and destruction caused by incoming shells. Despite these challenges, Anderson was not ready to give up the fort.

By afternoon, the first Union ships carrying reinforcements and supplies reached Charleston. But the ships could not approach the fort. If they had moved into the harbor, they would have been pounded by Confederate fire. The sailors could only watch the Confederate guns shoot at Fort Sumter.

As night fell, both sides stopped firing their artillery. But the next morning, the fighting began again. Thick, black smoke soon filled the sky over Fort Sumter, as another fire broke out. Beauregard's troops increased their

The Confederates' "ring of fire" surrounded the fort, and shells came from all directions.

S.S.BALTIC.OFF SANDY HOOK APR.EIGHTEENTH.TEN THIRTY A.M. .VIA

NEW YORK. . HON.S.CAMERON. SECY.WAR. WASHN. HAVING DEFENDED

FORT SUMTER FOR THIRTY FOUR HOURS UNTIL THE QUARTERS WERE EN

TIRELY BURNED THE MAIN GATES DESTROYED BY FIRE.THE GORGE WALLS

SERIOUSLY INJURED.THE MAGAZINE SURROUNDED BY FLAMES AND ITS

DOOR CLOSED FROM THE EFFECTS OF HEAT .FOUR BARRELLS AND THREE

CARTRIDGES OF POWDER ONLY BEING AVAILABLE AND NO PROVISIONS

REMAINING BUT PORK.I ACCEPTED TERMS OF EVACUATION OFFERED BY

GENERAL BEAUREGARD BEING ON SAME OFFERED BY HIM ON THE ELEV

ENTH INST.PRIOR TO THE COMMENCEMENT OF HOSTILITIES AND MARCHED

OUT OF THE FORT SUNDAY AFTERNOON THE FOURTEENTH INST.WITH

COLORS FLYING AND DRUMS BEATING.BRINGING AWAY COMPANY AND

PRIVATE PROPERTY AND SALUTING MY FLAG WITH FIFTY GUNS. ROBERT

ANDERSON.MAJOR FIRST ARTILLERY.COMMANDING.

Major Anderson sent this telegram to the secretary of war to inform him of the attack at Fort Sumter.

attack. Around one o'clock, a Confederate shot knocked down the fort's flagpole.

Taking down a fort's flag is a sign of surrender. Some Southern troops thought Union soldiers had taken down their flag and were giving up. For several hours, the guns fell silent. Beauregard sent messengers to talk to Anderson. But by the time they arrived, the U.S. flag once again flew over Fort Sumter. Still, Anderson realized that he and his men could not continue to fight. He finally agreed to turn over Fort Sumter to Confederate troops. In return, Beauregard let the Union troops leave peacefully and return north.

AFTER THE BATTLE

News of the surrender quickly spread through Charleston. Most people were glad the fighting was over. Confederate troops rowed over to Fort Sumter and talked with Union soldiers there. One Union soldier later wrote, "Many of the South Carolina officers … who were formerly in our service, seemed to feel very badly at firing upon their old [friends] and flag." Governor Pickens, however, was

A few days after the Union surrendered the fort, Southern sightseers came to see the place where the war began.

thrilled with the Confederate victory. He told the people of Charleston, "Your independence is won upon a glorious battlefield."

On April 14, 1861, Anderson and his men left Fort Sumter and sailed for New York. At the fort, the U.S. flag was lowered and the Confederate flag went up.

Despite the defeat at Fort Sumter, President Lincoln made preparations to end the uprisings in the South. On April 15, he said the Confederate states were ignoring the nation's laws. He asked for 75,000 soldiers to help end the rebellion in those states. In the North, volunteers quickly stepped forward to fight.

Meanwhile, eight more slave states debated whether to stay in the Union or join the Confederacy. Four decided to stay in the Union, while the other four joined the Confederacy.

In the North, some people thought the war would end quickly. The Union had more people than the Confederacy. It also had more factories to make military

An 1861 illustration shows the scene at a military recruitment center in New York.

supplies. However, Southern troops believed they were fighting for an important cause. In July, nearly 2,800 Union soldiers were killed, injured, or captured in a defeat at the First Battle of Bull Run. Northerners then realized that the end would not come soon.

The Civil War dragged on, and hundreds of thousands of soldiers died on both sides. Fort Sumter was the site of more battles. In 1863, Union ships entered

The Union attack on Fort Sumter in 1863

Charleston Harbor and fired at both Sumter and Moultrie. That same year, the Union Army tried to attack Charleston by land. Both efforts failed, and the Confederacy kept control of Fort Sumter.

Finally, late in 1864, Northern troops advanced through Georgia. By this time, the South was close to defeat. Residents and Confederate troops fled Charleston. In February 1865, Union troops entered the city and soon took back Fort Sumter. Less than two months later, the government held a special ceremony at the fort. The same U.S. flag that had flown during the battle of April 1861 was once again raised over the fort. This ceremony marked the end of the war and the historic role Fort Sumter had played in it.

Today, Fort Sumter is a national monument.

GLOSSARY

artillery—large guns, such as cannons, that require several soldiers to load, aim, and fire

Cabinet—a president's group of advisers who are the heads of government departments

civil war—war between opposing groups within one country

Constitution—the document that describes the basic laws and principles by which the United States is governed

economy—the way a region runs its industry, trade, or finance

militia—military force, often made up of local volunteers

reinforcements—a new supply of troops to strengthen a military force

shell—a metal container filled with gunpowder and fired from a large gun

Union—the United States of America; also the Northern states that fought against the Southern states in the Civil War

DID YOU KNOW?

- In 1861, the Confederates attacked Fort Sumter for a total of 34 hours. More than 3,000 artillery shells were fired at the fort.

- No soldiers on either side were killed during the two-day battle at Fort Sumter in April 1861. It is possible, however, that some slaves working at Fort Moultrie died during the fighting.

- Union Major Robert Anderson had been Confederate General P.G.T. Beauregard's artillery instructor at the U.S. Military Academy at West Point, New York.

- The special barge that the South built to attack Fort Sumter was called a floating battery. It was about 100 feet (30.5 meters) long and was covered with iron. The barge had no power of its own and had to be towed into position.

- Union officer Abner Doubleday is most famous for something he never did. In 1905, a special committee said that Doubleday had invented baseball in 1839. Historians now know this is not true.

IMPORTANT DATES

Timeline

1829
Work begins on Fort Sumter in Charleston Harbor.

1860
In November, Abraham Lincoln is elected president of the United States; in December, South Carolina secedes from the Union and Major Robert Anderson moves Union troops from Fort Moultrie to Fort Sumter.

1861
In January, South Carolina gunners turn back a Union ship trying to bring supplies to Fort Sumter; in February, Southern states that have seceded from the Union form the Confederate States of America; in April, President Lincoln sends supplies and troops to Fort Sumter; on April 12, Confederate forces attack the fort; on April 14, Major Anderson surrenders Fort Sumter.

1863
The North launches the first of several attacks to retake Fort Sumter and the city of Charleston.

1865
In February, Union forces retake Fort Sumter; in April, the Civil War ends.

Important People

Robert Anderson (1805–1871)
Major who commanded Union troops at Fort Sumter in 1861

Abner Doubleday (1819–1893)
Union captain at Fort Sumter

P.G.T. Beauregard (1818–1893)
Confederate general who led the attack on Fort Sumter

James Buchanan (1791–1868)
U.S. president at the time South Carolina seceded from the Union

Abraham Lincoln (1809–1865)
U.S. president whose election led South Carolina to secede and who fought the Civil War to keep the Union whole

Jefferson Davis (1808–1889)
President of the Confederate States of America

Francis Pickens (1805–1869)
Governor of South Carolina during the attack on Fort Sumter

WANT TO KNOW MORE?

At the Library

Anderson, Dale. *The Causes of the Civil War.* Milwaukee: World Almanac
Library, 2004.

Colbert, Nancy A. *The Firing on Fort Sumter: A Splintered Nation Goes to
War.* Greensboro, N.C.: Morgan Reynolds, Inc., 2001.

Lassieur, Allison. *James Buchanan: America's 15th President.* New York:
Children's Press, 2004.

McPherson, James M. *Fields of Fury: The American Civil War.* New York:
Atheneum Books for Young Readers, 2002.

Slavicek, Louise Chipley. *Abraham Lincoln.* Philadelphia: Chelsea House
Publishers, 2004.

On the Web

For more information on *Fort Sumter*, use FactHound
to track down Web sites related to this book.

1. Go to *www.facthound.com*

2. Type in a search word related to this book
   or this book ID: 0756516293

3. Click on the *Fetch It* button.

Your trusty FactHound will fetch the best Web sites for you!

On the Road

Fort Sumter National Monument
1214 Middle St.
Sullivan's Island, SC 29482
843/883-3123
The site of the first battle of the Civil War

South Carolina Confederate Relic Room and Museum
Columbia Mills Building
301 Gervais St.
Columbia, SC 29201
803/737-8095
Displays of uniforms, flags, and weapons from the Civil War

Look for more We the People books about this era:

The Assassination of Abraham Lincoln
ISBN 0-7565-0678-6

The Battle of Gettysburg
ISBN 0-7565-0098-2

Battle of the Ironclads
ISBN 0-7565-1628-5

The Carpetbaggers
ISBN 0-7565-0834-7

The Emancipation Proclamation
ISBN 0-7565-0209-8

The Gettysburg Address
ISBN 0-7565-1271-9

Great Women of the Civil War
ISBN 0-7565-0839-8

The Lincoln–Douglas Debates
ISBN 0-7565-1632-3

The Missouri Compromise
ISBN 0-7565-1634-X

The Reconstruction Amendments
ISBN 0-7565-1636-6

Surrender at Appomattox
ISBN 0-7565-1626-9

The Underground Railroad
ISBN 0-7565-0102-4

A complete list of We the People titles is available on our Web site:
www.compasspointbooks.com

INDEX

About the Author

Michael Burgan is a freelance writer for children and adults. A history graduate of the University of Connecticut, he has written more than 90 fiction and nonfiction children's books for various publishers. For adult audiences, he has written news articles, essays, and plays. Michael Burgan is a recipient of an Educational Press Association of America award.